Throwing the Perfect Shower

Throwing the Perfect Shower:

12 Themed Wedding and Baby Celebrations

Jill Williams Grover

Sterling Publishing Co., Inc. New York
A Sterling/Chapelle Book

Chapelle, Ltd.:

Owner: Jo Packham
Editor: Laura Best

Photography: Kevin Dilley, Hazen Photography
Hand-painted Illustrations:
   Shauna Mooney Kawasaki
Staff: Areta Bingham, Kass Burchett, Ray Cornia,
   Marilyn Goff, Karla Haberstich,
   Holly Hollingsworth, Susan Jorgensen,
   Emily Kirk, Barbara Milburn, Karmen Quinney,
   Caroll Shreeve, Cindy Stoeckl, Kim Taylor,
   Sara Toliver, Desirée Wybrow

If you have any questions or comments, please contact:
   Chapelle, Ltd., Inc.,
   P.O. Box 9252, Ogden, UT 84409
   (801) 621-2777 • (801) 621-2788 Fax
   e-mail: chapelle @chapelleltd.com
   web site: chapelleltd.com

Library of Congress Cataloging-in-Publication Data

Grover, Jill Williams.
   Throwing the perfect shower : 12 themed wedding and
baby celebrations / Jill Williams Grover.
         p. cm.
   "A Sterling/Chapelle book. "
   Includes index.
   ISBN 0-8069-9285-9
1.   Showers (Parties)   I. Title.
GV1472.7.S5 G76 2003
793.2--dc21   2002015878

 10 9 8 7 6 5 4 3 2 1

Published by Sterling Publishing Co., Inc.
387 Park Avenue South, New York, NY 10016
©2003 by Jill Williams Grover
Distributed in Canada by Sterling Publishing
c/o Canadian Manda Group, One Atlantic Avenue, Suite 105
Toronto, Ontario, Canada M6K 3E7
Distributed in Great Britain by Chrysalis Books
64 Brewery Road, London N7 9NT, England
Distributed in Australia by Capricorn Link (Australia) Pty. Ltd.
P.O. Box 704, Windsor, NSW 2756, Australia

Printed in China
All Rights Reserved

Sterling ISBN 0-8069-9285-9

*Dedicated to my children
Levi, Laci & River...*

my inspiration

Introduction

This shower book offers both traditional and unique ideas for a variety of festive events celebrating marriage as well as happy additions to the families of new babies. Upcoming weddings and the arrival of long-awaited babies are joyful occasions to share with loved ones of all ages. Here you will find suggestions to please everyone you invite. There are unique theme ideas for each guest of honor: bride, groom, infant, sibling, mom, dad, and grandma. Be certain guests feel the excitement of the shower as soon as they walk into the hosting home. Do make the shower as enjoyable for you as it is for your guests.

Prepare early because a happy and relaxed hostess is the best party giver. Bridal and baby showers are the most successful when a theme is chosen. The theme may determine the type of gifts to bring and clothing to wear. Keep the decorations festive and inviting and stay with the party colors wherever possible.

When planning the shower, be conscious of the new bride's or new mother's taste. Select foods, party favors, and gifts to her liking. Supply games and activities to entertain and involve all of the guests.

Once preparations are complete and everyone has arrived, spend the time enjoying the event with the honored guest and other loved ones. Introduce guests to one another and mingle to make certain guests feel welcome and comfortable.

Using the ideas in this book, feel free to change colors and use alternative materials to fit your personality and your special-occasion theme, then let the magic happen.

Enjoy!

Jill W. Grover

Contents

Wedding Showers 8

Baby Showers 60

Wedding

Showers

The celebration of an engagement is a romantic occasion to be shared with the family and close friends of the couple. In the event family and friends of the guests of honor have not met before, it is a great opportunity to bring everyone together in a relaxed atmosphere for the first time.

Engagement Shower

Plan a dinner to formally announce the engagement of the couple and celebrate their future together. Invite a small, personal guest list to a candlelight dinner.

The guests of honor should be involved in the plans for this type of shower, such as where it should be held, the style of shower, and the compatible couples who should attend, whether married or single with a date.

A video of this cherished time for family and close friends of the couple would be especially appropriate because of the variety of special toasts to be given. Note on the invitation "As a surprise we would like each guest to prepare a toast to offer the bride and groom."

left: Embellish a purchased card to add personality.

1. Cover card with a piece of organza fabric. Using a sewing machine, sew around edges to secure.

2. Inside the card write the specifics of the shower including theme to help guests select their "perfect" gift.

3. Add ribbon and shiny clear tinsel inside the card.

left & right: Place a decorated mirror on the front door.

1. Make decorative engagement rings by adding clear craft jewels to the prongs of gold ¾" cafe curtain rings.

2. String "rings" on a ribbon at the front and secure ribbon ends to back of mirror.

• These decorative rings also make party favors when placed in a small draw string pouch.

above: Build a treat plate for guests to enjoy.

1. Stack plates on top of one another supported by an upside-down bowl.

2. Fill largest plate with purchased raspberry wedding cookies.

3. Fill small plate with ribbon-wrapped bundles of cookies.

right:
• Layer table with two queen-size fitted sheets over a full-length tablecloth. Bunch parts of top layer and pin on small bouquets of silk flowers.

above:

- Breadsticks in a water pitcher make a creative serving idea.

- Have the couple's favorite foods served as snacks.

- Have plenty of fresh, colorful flowers.

left: Have each guest share "words of wisdom" with the engaged couple.

1. Supply paper and pens for guests to write down their words of wisdom and advice to the new couple.

2. Roll each paper into a scroll and tie with a ribbon.

3. Drop scrolls into a decorative bottle for couple to take home with them and share when they are alone.

left: Supply different-colored jeweled bracelets for guests to wrap around their goblet stems. This helps guests easily identify which glass is theirs. The bracelet also makes a great take-home party favor.

below left:
• Use a jeweled butterfly napkin ring as a gift-wrap topper.

• Shiny boxes secured with bright red sequin strings can hold foiled chocolates.

below center:
• Place cards can be a photograph of each guest.

below right:
• Make napkin rings from large plastic ruby-red rings and blue-beaded bracelets.

Selecting a specific theme simplifies the planning and provides a focal point for all of the party elements. Special holidays such as Valentine's Day already have distinct colors and decorations traditionally defined.

Valentine Bridal Shower

A crisp red-and-white party sets the mood for a bridal shower filled with hearts and wishes for "happy ever after." Guests will enjoy the excitement of this type of wedding shower, whether it is thrown in February or not. A party themed with hearts, cupids, and soft music is certainly appropriate for a bridal shower.

To keep costs of the shower within your budget, when collecting decorations for this event, take advantage of the red-closeout sales after Christmas or Valentine's Day. Shiny tinsel, candy canes, red-and-white tablecloths, bell-trimmed glasses, and red plates can make for a festive shower.

above: Create a colorful Valentine invitation.

1. Cut white card stock to desired size.

2. Using a glue stick, adhere foil wrapping paper, rhinestones, and sequins to create the party dress of your dreams.

3. For an extra touch, adhere wrapping paper to the envelope flap.

4. Write necessary shower information inside, including where the bride has registered.

above: Design a gift bag to hold the invitation.

1. Adhere a shiny foil heart to the front of a gift bag.

2. Wrap invitation in tissue paper, tie with colored tinsel, and place in gift bag.

3. Hang gift bag on guest's doorknob.

above & right: Make a wreath for the front door to greet guests as they arrive.

1. Using fine wire, secure framed photographs to a grapevine wreath. Use engagement pictures of the honored couple or wedding pictures of those attending the shower.

2. Work red-beaded wire into heart shapes and secure to the wreath.

3. Suspend wreath with several lengths of "love" ribbon.

above: Love letters are thoughtful party favors. The guests' delight is worth the time it takes to prepare them.

1. A month before the shower, contact husbands and boyfriends of your guests. Ask them to mail love letters to your home, honoring your guests.

2. Stack the letters for each guest together in a bundle on top of a box of chocolates.

3. Place letters and chocolates on the chair of each guest for a wonderful surprise.

left: Create unique centerpieces by adding framed pictures to purchased red heart topiaries.

below: Display romantic cards prominently to create a memorable mood.

1. String rhinestone-beaded ribbon across a large mirror mounted on the wall.

2. Attach a variety of new or saved red-and-white cards to ribbon with red clips.

left: Trim the serving tablecloth with tinsel.

1. Attach chunky tinsel with safety pins to tablecloth edge.

2. Wrap table legs with wrapping paper and secure with tape.

3. Display bride's gifts under the table until time to open them.

right: Make a place card to be placed on each guest's chair.

1. "Frame" place card with fake red jewels and clear plastic "crystal" shapes for extra pizazz.

2. Tie a frame to the back of each chair, as at right, with chunky tinsel.

3. Allow guests to take place cards home as charming keepsakes of the bridal shower.

• As an option, cover a cottage-cheese carton lid with a glued-on circle of paper for the name area. Add pleated or gathered ribbon as a frame for this place card.

below:

• Place red or white carnations in small vases.

• Buy a professionally decorated cake such as this one with malted milk balls and shaved chocolate, or use the photograph as a guide to decorate your own.

above:

• Use a large paper valentine for a place mat at each table setting.

• Red bangle bracelets used as napkin rings make a fun party favor to wear instantly.

• Take advantage of after-Christmas closeout sales to purchase candy canes and other red candies. Hot-glue wrapped candy canes together to form a heart. Add a ribbon, and use as an edible decoration.

above:

• Cookies fit perfectly in a tubular flower vase.

• Wrap ribbon around candles and place them in interesting vases or goblets filled with chocolates or red hots. Only keep ribbon-wrapped candles lit for an hour to prevent ribbon from burning.

top right:

• Introduce a "hot" aroma by sprinkling red hots over the top of a votive.

• Color-copy photographs and punch out in heart shapes to place around table with shiny red sequins.

above:

• Invite the sound of wedding bells by attaching leather bands with jingle bells to glasses.

• Fill ice-tray sections with maraschino cherries. Divide cherry juice evenly between sections. Top off sections with water. Freeze until solid.

An all-girl formal bridal shower can be held. In the invitations invite guests to come dressed in their finest attire to enjoy the good things in life.

A Formal Affair

When choosing decorations, include an appealing arrangement of beautiful flowers, candles, linens, and food that tastefully conveys an atmosphere of sophisticated refinement.

To add warmth and a bit of personality, unconventional colors or patterns may be used. Though a checkered pattern is not generally associated with a formal celebration, keying a theme to a checkered pattern offers an unassuming flavor to a black-and-white formal event—making guests feel more comfortable.

Supply beautiful music and an array of fancy, tempting foods for guests to enjoy in a candle light setting, even if the shower is held in the late afternoon. The ambiance of romance sets the party mood.

You will marry prince ch...

above: Make a formal invitation.

1. Buy an appropriate invitation to embellish.

2. Add a ribbon with printed words.

3. Sprinkle star glitter inside invitation before placing in envelope.

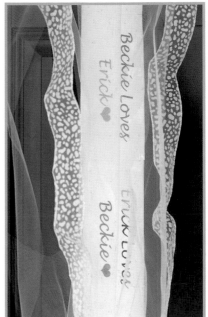

above & left: Wrap front door to look like a wedding gift.

1. Make the banner, using a computer software program. Keep your party message clear and concise. Make the banner long enough to run horizontally and vertically on the front door.

2. Laminate the banner to protect it from the weather.

3. Secure banner with tape on edges of the door.

4. Run wide, sheer ribbon over the banner. Make a large bow from the same ribbon and adhere to the "gift."

above: Make elegant place cards.

1. Cut desired squares out of card stock.

2. Write guests' names on fronts with permanent marker.

3. Adhere sequin ribbon to front of cards.

4. Secure place cards in purchased silver place card holders.

left: Coordinate a centerpiece that will complement the rest of the setting.

1. Arrange your choice of flowers in a favorite vase. Position flowers above or below eye level so as not to obstruct someone's view.

2. Float preprinted silk ribbon in vase.

above: Add live music to a formal shower.

right: Cover chairs with sheer fabric.

1. Measure and cut fabric piece to cover seat.

2. Cut sheer fabric to twice the circumference of the seat and the height of the seat plus 1½". Gather-stitch onto seat cover.

3. Sew a 1" hem along the material to cover chair legs.

4. Cut length for bow. Sew ¼" hem along the edge.

• Use a vintage lapel pin to scallop the hems of layered tablecloths.

above: Add a spider mum to the top of professionally decorated cake.

left & right: Make a wedding garland.

1. Run strings of beads across a mantel.

2. Attach garters, heart sachets, and anything lacy and white, using earrings and vintage jewelry.

above left: Make unique napkin rings from vintage bowties.

above right: Scatter silver bells on the tabletop.

left: Use a crystal votive candleholder as a dessert cup. Serve chocolate cookies or vanilla ice cream.

Cube Diagram

above: Make party favor holders, using four cards to form each frame.

1. Referring to the Cube Diagram at the left, punch four holes in each card, using a one-hole punch.

2. Lace a ribbon through holes. Tie one card to another to form a square.

3. Tuck tissue paper inside holder.

4. Place a small gift such as a candle or piece of candy in tissue.

37

A princess party can remind your guests how special they are and let them know how much they mean to you.

Princess Party

This special shower is decorated purely in white. From napkins and plates to decorations and party favors keep everything white, fluffy, soft, and inviting. Use your best china and crystal tableware. Sheer, white fabrics with sheen will add a bit of regal elegance.

Rhinestones and clear costume jewelry such as bracelets, and necklaces add glamour to the decorations. White tulle wrapped around candles and white lace handkerchiefs bring an elegant touch.

To add to the ambience of this bridal shower, guests may be asked to dress up in attire befitting a fairy-tale princess. Have available extra pairs of gloves, boas, silk wraps, and costume jewelry for the guests and bride-to-be to wear. She and her guests will enjoy "being" princesses.

Crown Pattern

above: Create a "royal" invitation.

1. Using the Crown Pattern, draw a simple crown with a pencil on a separate paper. Glue rhinestones and glitter onto crownlines and points.

2. Fold white card stock into a card. Cut a square out of the center front of card just large enough to frame the crown. Glue crown inside card. Glue bow to front of card.

3. Handwrite shower information inside card.

right: Embellish a simple spiral tree to use as a decoration.

1. Set up a white Christmas tree in a designated area of party room. Wrap the center pole with a white boa.

2. Add some tulle casually hanging down the middle. Decorate tree with a fluffy garland, ornaments, and ribbon.

right: Create a unique table.

1. Paint a wooden farm table white.

2. Adhere embossed wallpaper on top of table with wallpaper glue.

3. Buy a piece of decorative glass, cut to fit tabletop.

• Elegantly fold linen napkins and place on the plates to help enhance the table.

• Surprise guests by using a party favor to embellish each napkin. Purchase hair ribbons or lace clips to fasten around each napkin in place of a napkin ring.

• Although white is always appropriate, you may use colored linens to complement your china and decor.

• Bring out your best china, crystal, and silver. If you need to borrow from several people, either alternate the different patterns at each place setting or set different tables with their own matching pattern.

above & right: Embellish party chairs to appear as wedding dresses.

1. Purchase wedding gowns and veils from a local thrift shop. Cut gowns into as many useful pieces as possible.

2. Tack veils, tulle, and dress pieces to each chair.

3. Secure beads and sequins with hat pins, making removal easy after the shower is over and guests have departed.

right: Supplying tiaras for each guest to wear at the shower reminds them how beautiful and regal they all are.

• When preparing the table and party favors, opt for white and shiny articles.

• Make a place card by arranging a petite jewel-framed photograph of each guest on top of their plate.

• Decorate table with discount store crystal ashtrays filled with costume jewelry beads.

• Wrap white linen napkins with crystal beads.

• Display crystal Cinderella shoes as part of the place setting.

above: String jeweled necklaces and baubles around a chandelier to add more sparkle and decoration.

A Fall Shower

If your shower falls near a holiday, decorate the party to match the season. A natural way to celebrate in the autumn months is to take advantage of the beauty of a fall afternoon.

Set up the party table and chairs outside. Scatter fresh flowers and leaves on the grass. Use as many natural autumn materials in the decor as possible.

Have a backup plan in the event of inclement weather, such as pulling chairs and table onto a covered deck or under a canopy.

Depending on the type of group, plan activities they may enjoy while they are outdoors together. From jumping into a pile of leaves to playing croquet, or pairing unacquainted guests up with lists for following written clues to a scavenger hunt treasure, have options open for the guests to mingle with each other. Since Cinderella's pumpkin became a coach, imagine your own magic for party fun.

right: Gather doubled tulle and sew onto orange cotton tablecloth around perimeter of tabletop. Place pumpkins under table "skirt." Add fall leaves to enhance the ambience.

above: Embellish a purchased fall invitation to add personality.

1. Place invitation in a cellophane bag.

2. Add fresh fall leaves and tie top with ribbon.

3. Tape invitation to top of stick and push bottom of stick into a pumpkin. Add a ribbon.

4. Place invitation on guest's porch.

right: Add color and interest to the tablesetting with purchased gold or orange decorative trees.

above: Make unusual place cards.

1. Use Christmas ornaments such as this frog prince and gold dress. Wrap copper wire around ornament to fashion a holder.

2. Embellish place cards with sequins, flowers, and beads.

3. Write guests' names on small cards and place in wire holders.

right: Create an unusual way to serve drinks.

1. Make coasters from three canning jar lids stacked and hot-glued together.

2. Glue buttons, beads, and jewels around each jar rim.

3. Serve fresh grape juice in clean pint canning jars placed on coasters.

above: Display photograph of honored couple and be certain to take plenty of photographs of those attending the shower.

left:

• Wrap cookies with tulle and ribbon and place inside a colorful photograph box.

• String colored plastic beads on thin wire and run wires around table to add to the decorations.

above:

• Use colorful photograph boxes to hold crackers and cookies.

• Cover food plates with plastic wrap to protect. Place new decorative hats over plastic wrap to add to decor.

• Place a bottle of fresh grape juice inside a plaid sack for a fall party favor.

left: Make pizza snacks and serve with grapes, breads, cheeses, and fruit.

Groom's Party by the Bay

Traditionally, a bachelor party full of excessive celebrating and carousing is held for the groom-to-be by his friends. As an unexpected gift to the groom, the bride-to-be or her mother may throw the groom a quiet party by the bay.

With an upcoming busy schedule this "shower" is meant to bring comfort, relaxation, and recognition to the groom and his friends.

The party is set up in a location where the men can do activities they love to share together. Whether they enjoy the day fishing, biking, or hiking, they have a spot where they can come back to relax, eat, and play a friendly game of cards.

The view of the bay is the decoration, while nature sets the peaceful mood.

above: Create a rustic invitation.

1. Cut a square piece of cardboard and top with a square piece of tissue paper cut smaller than the cardboard. Add a piece of brown card stock with burnt edges and party information written on it.

2. Place a rusty nail through each corner to connect papers. Cut nail tips with a pair of wire cutters.

3. Fill back of each hole with hot glue to keep nail in place. Tie with jute.

4. Deliver invitations to the groom and his friends in a sack with jute tied around the handles.

above: Incense provides relaxation.

1. Fill rusty buckets with sand. Top sand with green lentil beans.

2. Place incense sticks in sand and light just before party begins.

right:

• Make a table by placing three 2' x 10' planks on top of two sawhorses.

• Provide lanterns for light as the party goes into the evening hours.

left:

• Use machinery parts as coasters and candleholders.

• After the party, the decorations of work gloves, clay pigeons, and scented bark candles become the party favors.

below: Have box lunches prepared with cookies, chips, and sandwiches. Top lunches with jute or raffia and tissue paper.

right:

• Serve drinks in colorful bottles, old canteens or thermos bottles.

• Place small containers of salsa, honey mustard, and sunflower seeds around the table.

• Peanuts and pistachios tossed around the table add to the decoration and can be eaten as well.

Baby

Showers

Pastel Pink & Baby Blue Shower

Trends are leading back to couples waiting for the birth of the baby to find out the sex. If the shower is held before the baby is born and the parents do not know the sex of the baby yet, a traditional pink-and-blue party celebrates the anticipated birth regardless of gender. This is also an appropriate shower for a twin boy and girl.

Invite family members and the mother's closest friends. The traditional baby shower tends to be the most relaxed gathering and the easiest to prepare for.

Traditionally showers were given by the expectant mom's mother. Parties are now more commonly hosted by extended family members, close neighbors, or coworkers. It is often cohosted by two or three people, which is less stressful and costly.

Though pink and blue are traditional baby colors, add pastel yellows, greens, and lavenders as well to signify new life. Represent chosen colors in the shower food, decorations, and party favors.

Brandon and Kassie
have a new
Baby Boy
Come see him at
the baby shower on
Saturday, April 6, 12:00

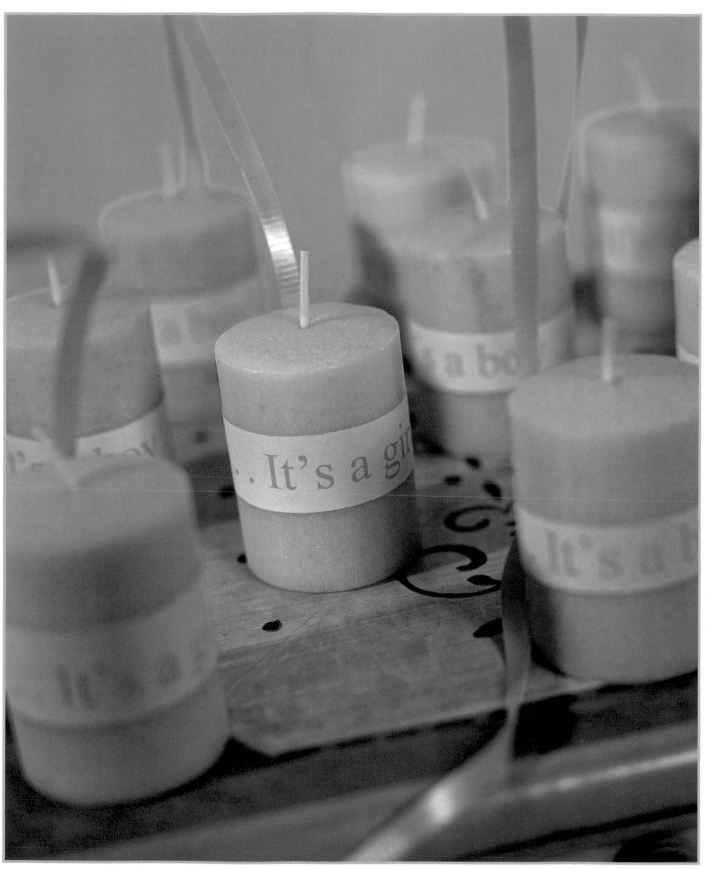

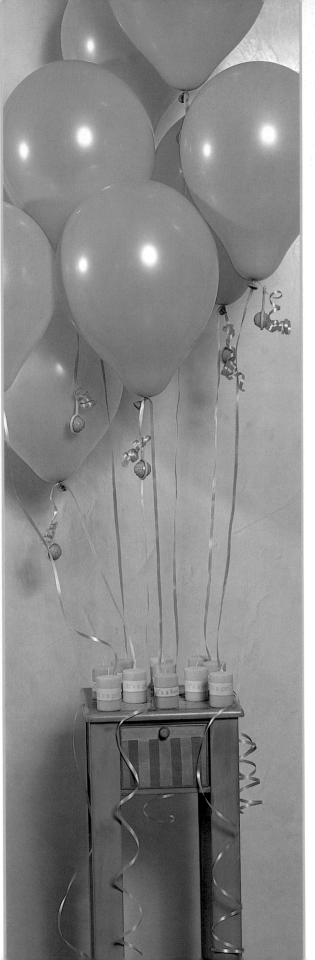

above: Create a simple pink-and-blue invitation.

1. Use images from coloring books, greeting cards, or children's original drawings. Be as creative as you like. The photo book on the left was color-copied and used for the invitation on the right.

2. Place two brightly colored papers underneath the copied cover and pin together with a diaper pin.

3. Write a welcoming message on the inside papers along with the shower information.

right: Make an eye-catching display to announce the party location.

1. Computer print or hand draw "it's a girl" or "it's a boy" banners. Wrap banners around petite candles and secure with a glue stick.

2. Tie a miniature rattle to curling ribbon and attach to a group of helium-filled balloons.

3. Before the party begins, place candles with balloons, a welcoming sign, and streamers on the front porch to help direct guests to the correct house.

left: Display family photographs wherever appropriate.

1. Obtain a photograph of the mother-to-be when she was a baby.

2. Mat and frame the photograph to match the colors and decor of the shower.

3. Display the photograph in the entryway to the party for guests to see in anticipation of what the new baby will look like.

4. Allow the mother to take the framed photograph home as a gift.

right: Embellish a large basket for guests to place their gifts in as they arrive.

1. Cover the basket handle with stuffed animals attached with wire.

2. Place basket by the front door before the shower begins.

3. When it is time to open gifts, take the basket full of gifts to the mother.

4. Let the new mother take the basket home to transport her new gifts in along with the stuffed animals for the new baby.

right: Decorate as many tables as needed for all guests to sit comfortably. If necessary, you may use one central table as the serving area and invite guests to take their food to a sitting room or outside to enjoy.

1. Wrap a card table similar to a present with wide wrapping paper. Secure wrapping paper underneath the table.

2. Wrap table legs with ribbon.

3. Add ribbon to corners and place a large bow in the center.

above & right: Incorporate original artwork in the party decor.

1. If the new baby has siblings, give them a few days before the party to make a special picture for the baby and display it as a decorative backdrop to the table.

2. If this is the first baby in the family, ask the children of the guests, or young relatives of the baby to make their own masterpiece to share at the shower.

3. Obtain and display drawings made by the mother-to-be when she was a child, as a tribute to her own life circle.

right: Make a colorful centerpiece by arranging silk flowers in a clear vase filled with party-colored jelly beans or wrapped chocolates.

right & below: Create place cards.
1. Cut baby items such as a pacifier or a bottle from baby-shower wrapping paper. Glue paper items onto colored card stock squares.

2. Hand-write guests' names on fronts of cards.

3. Glue cards to plastic diaper pins. Place in candy-filled containers.

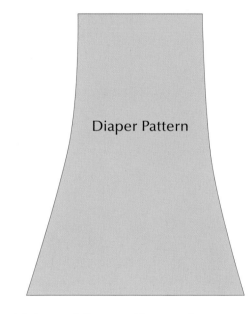

Diaper Pattern

left: Make a "diapered" container to use as a party favor or place card.

1. Using a copy machine, enlarge the Diaper Pattern above to fit your container.

2. Cut diaper from white flannel.

3. Hot-glue diaper sides around container. Glue a plastic safety pin on each side.

4. Fill container with cellophane grass and candy.

above:

• Use teething rings as napkin holders.

• Use embellished baby shoes as part of a centerpiece. Paint simple flower designs on old baby shoes and dye shoelaces to match.

above: Decorate baby sleepers by securing a colorful, soft boa with a simple running stitch to the collar and sleeve cuffs. Use embellished sleepers as decorations for the shower.

below: After the shower, remove the boa by gently pulling out the running stitch. Allow mother to take sleepers home as gifts when she leaves.

below: Make a nonedible decorative cake to display.

1. Using a craft knife, cut cake out of craft board.

2. Frost "cake" with cream or butter frosting and decorate as desired.

3. Display cake on a hat box. Embellish with ceramic baby trinkets. Wrap a baby-soft boa around the bottoms of the cake and hat box.

4. Serve a separate sheet cake to the shower guests.

• Add candles to pastel meringue cookies to give the appearance of miniature celebration cakes.

right: Use a child's party hat as a unique gift-wrap idea.

1. Hot-glue a boa to rim of child's party hat.

2. Cut a plastic party tablecloth into small squares to use as tissue paper.

3. Wrap a gift such as a rolled-up baby sleeper or blanket in a tablecloth square.

4. Tie tablecloth square closed with a pink bracelet or ribbon.

5. Insert the wrapped gift into a child's party hat.

left:

- Keep the table decorations "soft" in appearance.

- Use a boa as ribbon to top a baby gift.

- Candles add warmth to a setting; however, be careful to keep candles a safe distance away from decorations and other flammable materials.

- Use a votive candleholder to hold purchased pretzel sticks covered in pastel candy sprinkles.

- Fill glass serving dishes with pink- or blue-colored candies.

Star Diagram

left: Using shower theme colors, create party favors.

1. Fill cellophane bags with cotton candy.

2. Print the words "A star is born" on strips of paper and place visibly in bags.

3. Using the Star Diagram above, hot-glue five cotton swabs together forming a star.

4. Print baby's name and birth weight on paper strips.

5. Loop ribbon through a star and a strip of paper, then tie around each bag to close.

right: Incorporate the party favors in the decorations.

1. Fill a wire basket with cellophane grass and colorful party favors.

2. Hang stars around the basket edge.

3. Display basket on pastel-colored hat box until guests take party favors home.

Baby Snow Shower

It does not need to be the springtime to celebrate new life. Combine the winter season and the birth of a baby by throwing a Baby Snow Shower.

Use a large window or patio door as the backdrop to bring the season into the party without bringing in the cold to the guests. Decorate the room as if the party were outdoors by using a snow white or fleece tablecloth and sticking plastic snowflakes onto the windows.

When choosing the party colors, add a "springing to new life" touch to the dreary season by opting for bright colors which will stand out against a snowy background. Bright gift bags and colorful decorative items can be studded with delicate snowflakes for extra wintery dazzle.

There is
Snow Place
like a baby
Shower
Saturday : 1:00
Dress warm
and
Snuggly...

above: Create wintery invitations.

1. Purchase a decorative snowman sack for each guest. Using a color copier, photocopy sack onto white card stock. Trim edges.

2. Write shower details on back of card-stock invitation.

3. Place a wintery invitation inside each sack, along with snowflake confetti, before hand-delivering.

above & right: Create a cheerful welcome by decorating the front walkway. If the party is in the late afternoon hours, add strands of miniature lights to trees and shrubs around the entry.

1. Embellish colorful purchased paper and lacy stars with strands of garlands, costume jewelry, mittens, and ribbons.

2. Hang paper stars and ornaments on outside trees and bushes.

above: Set the dessert and party favor table in front of a large window or glass door to simulate an outdoor winter shower.

right:
• Make a handmade baby blanket, scarf, and hat for the baby on his ride home in the wintery weather.

• For the shower, the blanket doubles as the gift-table covering.

• The hat covers two round jars full of sugar cookies stacked on top of each other, creating a snowman cookie jar.

• A piece of fleece makes a scarf for the snowman's neck.

above Make a snowman hood.

1. Glue a black felt hat onto a purchased white furry hat.

2. Stitch to front of hat large and medium black pompoms for eyes and mouth. Sew on cloth carrot for nose.

right:

- Embellish the serving table with batting sprinkled with artificial snow.

- Serve salad toppers in bowls arranged like a snowman.

- Give the scarf as a gift to keep the baby warm on the drive home.

below: Make a snowman kit for the new mom to share with her baby.

1. Embellish a tall black hat with silk flowers.

2. Purchase a plastic carrot nose from a craft store. Use red coat buttons for the mouth and colorful earrings for buttons.

3. Paint aerosol-can lids black and white to use as eyes.

above: Decorate drinking glasses.

1. Moisten glass rims with a cut lemon.

2. Dip moist glass edges in colored sugar.

3. Fill glasses with wassail. Add lemons.

right:

- New hair clips keep napkins in tidy bundles.

- Serve coconut snowballs as a wintery treat.

- Foil balloon weights add charm.

above: Make "fruit people" to use as decorations.

1. Secure a lime head, orange middle, and grapefruit bottom together with enough toothpicks to keep them steady.

Option: Use an orange head, grapefruit middle, and pomelo grapefruit bottom.

2. Using straight pins, top fruit with a colorful new child's sock "hat" tied with ribbon.

3. Twist strands of yarn together to create a scarf for each neck. Tie ends in knot.

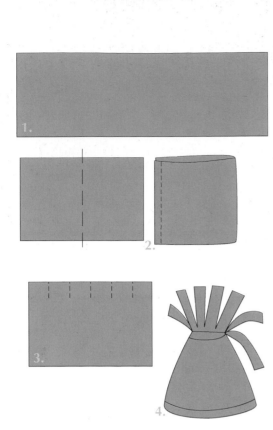

above: Make a baby hat.

1. Cut a rectangular piece of fleece the circumference of a baby's head plus 1".

2. Fold and sew into a tube shape.

3. Cut 1"-wide by 3"-deep slits at top end of tube. Knot adjoining strips together.

4. Tie a piece of fleece around the top of the tube. Roll up bottom edge of tube to form a cuff.

right: Make a baby blanket.

1. Use two differently patterned pieces of fleece fabric.

2. Lay fabrics together and cut 3–4" deep slits around fleece edges every 1–2". Tie fabric strips together in a knot. Note: A square piece will be cut away from each corner.

above: The only snow this snugly warm baby sees is the walk from the car to the front door in a take-home blanket and hat.

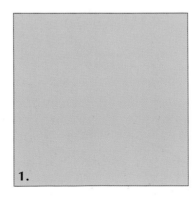

84

below: Use hand towels as napkins.

above: Make snowman party favors.

1. Place snowman-shaped lotion bottles in plastic bags. Sprinkle coconut into bags for snow. Tie tops with ribbons.

2. Use plastic Christmas bulbs as name tags. With marker, write each guest's name on the tags.

below: Prepare a "shoe full of treats" as a party favor.

1. Fill a plastic bag with candies and goodies.

2. Place treat bag in new colorful boots or shoes purchased at a discount shoe store for guests to take home.

New Sibling Shower

The focus of the New Sibling Shower is to honor not only the new baby and his mother but also the young child that has a new baby sibling.

Many times an older sister or brother feels left out when a new baby is brought into the family. This party allows the sibling the opportunity to be in the spotlight, which helps the child accept the new baby with happiness rather than jealousy.

The preparations for this party are simple. The idea is to have the young child help make the party decorations, food, and invitations. Let him or her feel useful in specific ways and needed as much as the new baby.

The new mother's friends and their children or the sibling's neighborhood friends and their parents make up the guest list. The activities for the shower bring guests of every age together to share a great time.

above: Help the older child make the invitations.

1. Photocopy a purchased or handmade child's postcard onto a heavy piece of card stock.

2. Let the young child handwrite party information inside. Be certain children and parents alike are invited.

3. Mail card in a large, bright-colored envelope or let child hand-deliver, accompanied by an adult.

above: Mount a chalkboard on the front porch to receive messages from visitors and to display announcements.

1. With mom's help let the older child embellish a chalkboard by gluing on artificial flowers, pieces of colorful wallpaper, and marbles.

2. Let children create their own drawings, such as the one to the right, and display them on the chalkboard as well.

3. Don't forget to post a flyer on the chalkboard proclaiming the arrival of the new baby.

right: Make a festive entry decoration.

1. Select a colorful wallpaper border and cut it into enough squares to make the desired length banner.

2. Punch a hole in two opposite sides of all squares, except the top and bottom squares, which only require one hole.

3. Lace squares together with ribbon.

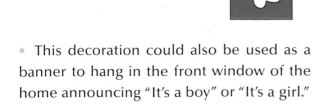

• This decoration could also be used as a banner to hang in the front window of the home announcing "It's a boy" or "It's a girl."

- Decorate a table to use as a serving table and accommodate mothers while children have their own setting on blankets on the ground.

- Layer and hot-glue a thrift shop bedskirt ruffle and cafe curtains to a tablecloth.

- On the table, place a photograph of the new baby being held by the older child.

91

below: Decorate table with pipe-cleaner flowers.

1. Roll pipe cleaners into spirals.

2. Run green pipe cleaner up through spiral center. Make a loop at top of stem to hold in place.

3. Display flowers in a pot filled with candies.

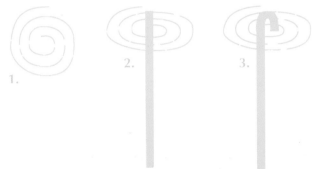

above: Make simulated baby bottles for party favors.

1. Cover empty toilet paper tubes with wrapping paper.

2. Wrap cellophane around bottoms of tubes and secure with pipe cleaners.

3. Fill each tube with small candies.

4. Top tubes with standard-sized baby bottle caps.

above: Make "play time" party favors for children to take home.

1. Using a cupcake pan, press a small ball of clay into a cupcake-holder shape.

2. Let clay dry, following manufacturer's instructions.

3. Use "clay cupcake holder" as a serving dish for a real cupcake in its paper liner decorated with pipe-cleaner designs.

- Fill empty lemonade cans with candy treats, a pipe cleaner flower, and a swizzle stick.

- Use animal photograph holders with guests' photographs as place cards.

- Give each child a dry-erase board and pens to make his own personalized place mat. Let each child take his mat masterpiece home as a party favor.

- Supply bath mitts to be used as erasers for place-mat drawings.

above:

- Scoop out the center of a cantaloupe or honeydew melon and add a scoop of colorful ice cream.

- Supply bowls of the children's favorite candies.

- Make a tray by cutting a piece of wrapping paper 3" larger than inside of a poster frame. Fold excess paper to back of poster cardboard and secure to back with tape.

left: Children love bright colors, so throw all the colors you can into this party. Keep the flavor of the party fun.

The shape, color, and style of the cake can be outrageous or traditional. If you are familiar with cake decorating and using fondant, this is an easy and colorful cake decorating idea because the shapes are simple.

If you are not familiar with working with fondant, take this design to a professional cake decorator, and let them work their magic, still showing your personality.

above: Supply unique hats purchased from a costume supply outlet. As children arrive at the party, allow them to choose a hat to wear throughout the day and take home as a party favor.

left: Young guests are invited to sit on beach towels and pillows surrounded by toy cars, dolls, balls, and stuffed animals.

Pink, Pink, Pink

Think pink. A shower with everything pink brings a soft, feminine feel to a baby girl's shower. Stuffed animals, flowers, lace, soft materials—all in a pink color make up the decorating elements.

If planning a shower for a boy baby, the general ideas can still apply by changing decoration, food, and gift colors to blue.

From decorations to food, and gifts to party favors, stay within the pink theme. This party is especially effective if the new nursery is also decorated in pink. Be certain to let guests know if this is the case so gifts can coordinate with the new baby's room decor.

Pink fabrics, beads, throw-away party items, and special keepsakes can be found that have pink accents to complement the shower colors. Porcelain dolls in pink dresses and tiny tea sets dotted with rosebuds can enhance a centerpiece on the party food table or theme a mantel focal point.

right: Make a pink bunny greeter.

1. Draw and cut out desired bunny from pink corrugated paper.

2. Glue bunny to heavy cardboard to make it sturdy enough to stand.

3. Cut three flowers from white corrugated paper. Hot-glue a smaller pink flower to the center of each white flower.

4. String flowers together with ribbon and tie around bunny's neck.

above: Embellish purchased cards to add personality.

1. Glue a strip of beads along inside edge of cards.

2. Place in velum envelopes and secure with bows.

below:

- Use collectible figurines such as a pink ballerina pincushion as part of the decor.

- Serve pink foods on pink dishes and pink drinks in pink glasses.

right: Make a fancy pink tablecloth.

1. Cut pink taffeta the size of the tabletop.

2. Measure tulle for the height of the table then double it. Fold the cut tulle in half lengthwise.

3. Place pink silk flowers between tulle layers. Sew edges of tulle around top edge of taffeta tablecloth.

4. Pin silk flowers and petals to the front of tulle layers.

above: Make pink place cards.

1. Cut place cards from rectangular pieces of pink floral paper. Embellish with buttons and write guests' names.

2. Put place cards in teacups filled with cellophane grass. Option: Embellish purchased place-card holders with glitter, buttons, and rhinestone jewels.

left:

- Make decorations that double as party favors.

- Wrap candles with beads. Secure with pink-headed pins.

- Sprinkle rose petals on tulle. Wrap tulle around votive and secure with ribbon.

- Display a framed photograph of the new baby.

- Tie paper napkins with new ponytail holders.

103

left:

- Decorate the table using a variety of pink and white items and party favors.

- Arrange a bouquet of pink and white roses in a pink container.

- Fill a large brandy snifter with purchased pink and white cookies.

- Serve sugar cookies in a baby's upside-down Easter hat filled with cellophane grass.

- Wrap a soft boa around dishes to add color.

right:

- Fill a jumbo baby bottle with pink mint chocolate chips and marshmallows. Wrap treats in a circle of tulle and tie with ribbon.

- Serve pink lemonade.

- Use pink silk flowers to top decorated cupcakes.

above:

• Embellish candles with strands of pearls.

• A beautiful, professionally decorated cake adds to a shower as the celebration of the "birth" day. If making your own cake, use white malt-ball candies cut in half and secure with frosting.

above: Decorate drink cans to hand out as birth announcements or serve as drinks for the party.

1. Cut floral wrapping paper 4" x 8½" and wrap around lemonade cans. Glue labels in place using a glue stick.

2. Attach a label such as "Happy 'Birth' Day AnnaLee" to the cans.

3. Wrap tulle ribbon around the cans and tie at the top.

right: Make pink party favors.

1. Fill plastic Easter eggs with white Jordan almonds.

2. Place eggs in a cellophane bag filled with pink Easter grass.

3. Attached purchased gift tags with guests' names printed on them.

above left:
- Place gifts in hat boxes, stack, and tie with tulle.

- Place a fluffy dress upside down in a colorful gift sack.

above right:
- Wrap a baby gift pillow between two place mats and tie together with a bow.

right:
- Fill a basket with rose petals and baby booties.

far right:
- Place baby socks in a jar. Top with a stuffed animal.

above: Stuff a decorative stocking with lotion, a baby bottle, pacifier, rattle, baby mittens, and soft wash cloths.

top right: Whether crocheted or sewed, hand-made baby booties will be cherished for years by the mother and baby.

bottom right: Mount a cherished outfit the new mom or dad wore as a baby to covered mat board and frame in the colors of the new nursery.

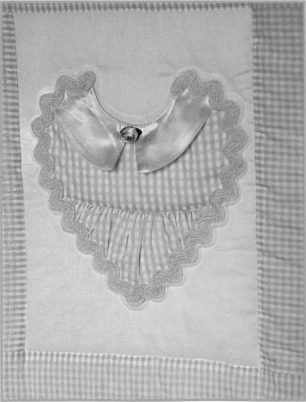

above & left: Make a quilt of cherished baby clothes worn by the new mom when she was a baby. Select items that are not in good enough condition to pass down to the new baby, but portions are salvageable enough for the quilt.

- Ruffles from her first dress

- Parts of colorful baby jumpers

- Baby shirts

- Holiday sweaters

- Favorite baby blankets

right: Bring clothing articles together in a collectible quilt.

1. Cut decorative pieces from cherished clothing articles. Cut nine equally sized squares of a coordinating material.

2. Sew cherished articles onto precut quilt squares. Each square may have a different clothing article attached.

3. Assemble the nine squares into a quilt with fabric strips running between each square.

Throw a baby shower for a new grandmother or those on both sides of the new baby's family. This party is a fun and friendly get-together that resounds with the joy of being a grandmother.

Grandma's Tea

Invite friends, neighbors, and her other grandchildren who will be happy to share in the excitement of the new baby's arrival. Wait until after the baby is born for this shower so the grandmother can show off the baby and have her first pictures of or with the baby developed and in hand to show as well.

A new grandmother needs to stock up on the necessities for when baby comes to visit. Delight "grandma" with helping gifts to care for her new grandbaby, such as diapers, bottles, and receiving blankets. A high chair, swing, or portable crib will also be appreciated to add to this new chapter in grandma's life.

above: Create "Springy" invitations.

1. Type party specifics on card stock. Tape a picture of the baby onto the card stock.

2. Sandwich card stock between decorative paper and velum.

3. Secure layers together with a ribbon looped through the papers.

4. Hot-glue a flower over ribbon bow.

right: Set up a garden party.

• Use a crisp white table covering and matching cloth napkins.

• Tie colorful ribbons around chair backs.

• Decorate with plenty of colorful flowers.

• Because children are invited, be certain there is ample seating for the adults and prepare a separate smaller table for the young set.

• Place small mementos and gifts on the chair of each invited guest.

above: Use purchased fondant to decorate your favorite sugar cookies. Scallop patterns can be made with sterile kitchen scissors and punches.

left:

• Serve cookies and treats in terra-cotta pots.

• Using permanent marker, write guest names on rims of miniature white pots for place cards.

right:

• Add fresh flowers to personally or professionally decorated cakes.

• Set table with heirloom dishes.

• Use chenille wire as napkin holders with flowers hot-glued on top.

left & above: Make party hats with the young guests.

1. Using decorative-edged scissors, cut out a circle twice the circumference of each child's head from white wrapping paper.

2. Place the circular paper on the child's head. Wrap a wire flower stem around the child's head to hold hat on comfortably.

3. Pull center of hat up through stem to make top rounder. Pinch tucks of paper to fit snugly.

4. Remove hat from head and hot-glue tucks together.

5. Place hat on child's head again and secure by wrapping a wire flower stem around the child's head.

right: Make party-favor baskets, using 12" plastic cups.

1. Cut rim off cup and save. Cut slits down sides of cup about 1" apart.

2. Using a pencil, roll 1" strips down around the cup.

3. Hot-glue cup ring to top of cup for basket handle.

4. Fill baskets with treats and trinkets.

below: Treat baskets and paper doll chains made at the party can also serve as decorations and party favors.

above: Create a party environment where you can make memories with your loved ones and laugh a lot.

left: Be certain to have activities to entertain the little ones while adults talk. Bubbles and bubble wands make the event enjoyable for all ages.

left: Let guests take their placecard flower home.

bottom left: Colorful photo albums can make fine gifts for the new grandmother as well as welcome party favors for guests.

bottom right: Stacked fragrant sachets can be used as party favors.

New Dad Golf Outing

Baby showers have traditionally been given for the expectant mother, but first-time daddy appreciates a party too. The new mom and her friends prepare a celebration for the new dad and his buddies.

This casual get together celebrates the occasion without the typical fancy decorations and games. Instead use the new daddy's hobby or favorite sport as a theme.

The wife and her friends make and send the invitations, and handle the arrangements. The new dad and his buddies are treated to a day of fun before he's introduced to his new "daddy" role.

For the new dad who loves to golf, a "shower" at the golf course is memorable. Plan to award trophies or prizes for "The longest drive," "Worst shot of the day," and "Closest to the hole."

Prepare food for after the golf round, whether in the club house, back at a home, or in a favorite restaurant. Even make party favors for the guys to take home after the party.

above: Make a golf style invitation.

1. Enlarge Golf Shirt Patterns on facing page 250%.

2. Cut Back out of heavy card stock.

3. Cut Inside out of white copy paper. Fold inward on dotted lines. Center and glue Inside on top of Back.

4. Cut Sides and Strip out of newspaper golf clippings.

5. Cut Sleeves and Bottoms out of a golf scorecard.

6. Cut Collars out of heavy blue paper.

7. Using all-purpose glue, assemble shirt parts on top of the folded white copy paper.

8. Hot-glue buttons down center.

9. Write party invitation details inside card. Hand-deliver to prospective party guests.

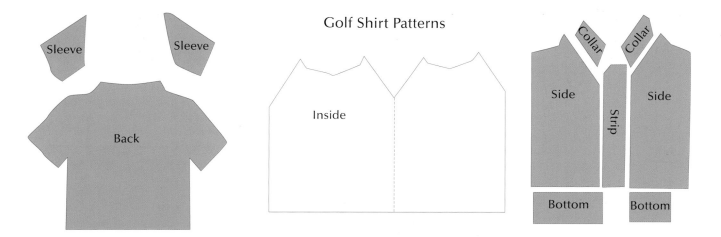

Golf Shirt Patterns

Sleeve

Sleeve

Back

Inside

Collar

Collar

Side

Side

Strip

Bottom

Bottom

above:

- Display golf-ball-shaped candies in a tray of wheat grass.

- A lemon meringue pie was set on a white bowl to give the idea of a golf ball.

- Fill a golf ball mug with white flowers.

above:

• Fill molded-fondant golf balls with pudding. Serve on a bed of wheat grass.

• Use glass candleholders as serving dishes.

right:

• Fill coffee mugs with bags of golf tees.

• Use airline bag tags as gift tags.

Special thanks to:

Jo Packham
Laura Best
Kevin Dilley
Cindy Heiser
Clyde, Sandy, Dustin,
   & Forrest Wohlgemuth
Ann & Kathy Williams
Mark Williams
Doug & Julie Grover
Erick & Beckie Griffiths
Heidi & Annee Farner
Tiffany & Montana Burnhope
Corey & Karine Waggoner
Bob & Lori Metcalf
Mike & Kitty Dunn
Creighton, Adrienne,
   & Chloe Thompson
Matt Davis
Alyson Korth
Rand Williams
Eagle Mountain Golf Course
Rod & Elaine Crockett
Joshua & Jaxon Edwards
Scott, Jennifer,
   & Raegan Uyematsu
Trekker Gray
Linda & Natalie Lowe
Steven & Kristy Chambers
Lisa Olson
Debbie Griffiths
All the staff at Chapelle, Ltd.

About the Author

Jill Grover, an interior designer, is the mother of three and resides with her husband and children in Northern Utah. She has appeared locally as well as nationally on various television programs, sharing advice on crafting and decorations. She has made use of her creative talents as the author of *Scary Scenes for Halloween, Handmade Giftwrap, Bows, Cards, and Tags* as well as *Dimestore Decorating*. She also plays the harp and makes really great chocolate chip cookies.

Index

Conversion Chart		
inches	mm	cm
⅛	3	0.3
¼	6	0.6
⅜	13	1.3
½	16	1.6
⅝	19	1.9
¾	22	2.2
⅞	25	2.5
1	32	3.2
1¼	38	3.8
1½	44	4.4
2	51	5.1
2½	64	6.4
3	76	7.6
3½	89	8.9
4	102	10.2
4½	114	11.4
5	127	12.7